THE FIELD GUIDE ON HOW TO

BE. MORE.

BREWDOG.

THE FIELD GUIDE ON HOW TO

BE. MORE.

BREWDOG.

This guide is the property of

....

EBURY
PRESS

1 3 5 7 9 10 8 6 4 2

Published in 2020 by Ebury Press an imprint of Ebury Publishing,
20 Vauxhall Bridge Road,
London SW1V 2SA

Ebury Press is part of the Penguin Random House group of
companies whose addresses can be found at
global.penguinrandomhouse.com

Book Design by www.Hampton.Agency

All photographs © BrewDog

www.penguin.co.uk

A CIP catalogue record for this book is available from the British
Library

ISBN 9781529106855

Printed and bound in Italy by L.E.G.O S.p.A

Penguin Random House is committed
to a sustainable future for our business,
our readers and our planet. This book is
made from Forest Stewardship Council®
certified paper.

This book is dedicated to all of our amazing
Equity Punks.

We are lucky to have over 100,000 amazing
shareholders from all over the world.

They are our community, our friends and
the heart and soul of our little business.

And this book, and everything we do,
is for them.

CONTENTS

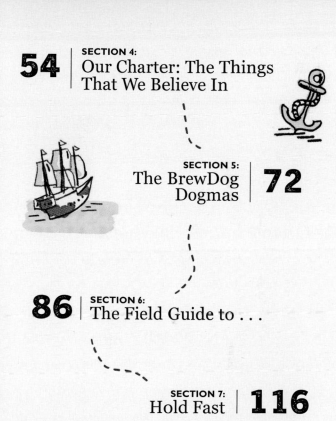

Bite the hand.

Dare to question.

Celebrate your victories.

Respect your beginnings.

Grow like hell.

Have no fear.

Share the profits.

Hack the system.

Own your failures.

Keep your promises.

Snap your leash.

Blaze your trail.

Slingshot your shiny pebble right between
the giant's eyes.

And for the love of god.

Brew your own goddamn beer.

HELLO, AND WELCOME TO OUR WORLD

'Here's to the crazy ones, the misfits, the rebels, the troublemakers, the round pegs in the square holes. Because the ones who are crazy enough to think that they can change the world, are the ones who do.'
Steve Jobs

BrewDog exists for one very simple reason, to make other people as passionate about great craft beer as we are. This has been our unerring mission since day one.

We want to put the passion, the taste, the artisan craftsmanship back into people's beer glasses and turn the global beer scene on its head.

We also want to show that craft beer can be a force for good in the world and build a completely new type of business. A business that is part community owned, a business that gives back, a business that is open and transparent and a business that looks after its amazing people incredibly well. In short, a business that we are all extremely proud to be a part of.

Our approach has been non-conformative and anti-authoritarian from the word go as we tore up the rule book and did things on our own terms. As we continue to grow, it is vitally important we stay true to the ethos and the principles that have gotten us this far.

For our amazing team members all over the world, this book is a reminder that we need to continue to not give a damn, continue to wear our heart on our sleeve and continue steadfastly on our mission to change the world of beer forever. This book contains tools to help us do just that.

For anyone else reading this book, it is a snapshot into the culture, the strategy and the alternative mindset of a business which has gone from two humans and a dog in 2007 to over 2,000 team members today and has already made a serious impact in the worlds of both beer and business.

Craft beer for the people,

James, Ellon, 2019

SECTION I. SECTION I. SECTION I. SECTION I.

Section 1

THE JOURNEY

2006

THE BEGINNING

Armed with a cobbled together 50L brew kit in Martin's mum's garage we (James and Martin) set out to recreate our favourite beer at the time, Sierra Nevada Pale Ale. We could not find many beers we wanted to drink in the UK back then so we decided the best thing to do was to brew our own. In October we met the legendary beer expert Michael Jackson (not the pop star!) and we let him taste a whisky barrel aged stout we had made at home. He tasted it, put the glass down slowly, looked us squarely in the eyes and told us to quit our jobs and start making beer full time. So we did.

2007

TEAM MEMBERS:	BEER BREWED:	SHARE HOLDERS:	BREWDOG BARS:
2 + 1 Dog	1,050 HL	2	0

In April 2007, in a derelict shed, on a godforsaken and dystopian industrial estate in Fraserburgh, BrewDog came howling into the world. We set up one tiny brewery with one very big mission: to make other people as passionate about great beer as we are. The first beer we ever brewed was Punk IPA, and that is still our flagship beer today. We brewed tiny batches, filled bottles, sold our beer at local farmers markets and more often than not spent our nights at the brewery too, either filling bottles or snoozing on sacks of malt on the floor.

BRACKEN

2008

TEAM MEMBERS:	BEER BREWED:	SHARE HOLDERS:	BREWDOG BARS:
9 + 1 Dog	4,050 HL	2	0

Things started getting crazy for us in 2008 and they've stayed crazy ever since. We masterminded the UK's strongest ever beer, Tokyo, resulting in a huge media storm and – if you believe the headlines – the downfall of Western civilisation. Despite this, we started exporting to Sweden, Japan and America and we told some lies to a bank so we could get some money to buy our first proper bottling machine.

2009

TEAM MEMBERS:	BEER BREWED:	SHARE HOLDERS:	BREWDOG BARS:
24 + 1 Dog	9,500 HL	1,329	0

This was the year we launched our alternative business model: Equity for Punks. In a groundbreaking first, we did crowdfunding before crowdfunding was even a thing and offered people the opportunity to buy shares in BrewDog online and over 1,300 Equity Punks invested. We also continued to push boundaries by brewing the world's strongest ever beer – Tactical Nuclear Penguin – at 32%, we aged a beer on a fishing boat and continued expanding our ramshackle brewery.

2010

TEAM MEMBERS:	BEER BREWED:	SHARE HOLDERS:	BREWDOG BARS:
39 + 1 Dog	15,800 HL	1,329	1

Opening our first craft beer bar in our home town of Aberdeen was a dream come true, and we were blown away by the response from our community. We held our first AGM for our Equity Punk shareholders, picked up the Gold Medal for Hardcore IPA at the World Beer Cup, and brewed a 55% abv (alcohol by volume) beer packed in roadkill, fusing art, craft beer and taxidermy to make it the world's most expensive beer ever.

2011

TEAM MEMBERS:	BEER BREWED:	SHARE HOLDERS:	BREWDOG BARS:
67 + 1 Dog	26,750 HL	6,567	4

After BrewDog Aberdeen worked out kind of ok, we opened bars in Glasgow and Camden. In true BrewDog style we announced our arrival in the capital by driving down Camden High Street in a tank. We brewed a beer at the bottom of the ocean, dispensed a 28% abv beer from a modified deer's head and started building our eco-brewery. We also welcomed over 5,000 new shareholders, raising over £2.2 million with our second round of Equity for Punks.

2012

TEAM MEMBERS:	BEER BREWED:	SHARE HOLDERS:	BREWDOG BARS:
135 + 1 Dog	36,500 HL	6,567	10

Our brand new brewery opened its doors in Ellon, ready to brew more craft beer than ever before. We also opened six new BrewDog bars, launched the phenomenal Dead Pony Club and grew revenues by 95%, prompting the *Sunday Times* Fast Track 100 to name us the UK's fastest growing food and drink company. Not bad considering we also projected ourselves naked onto the Houses of Parliament.

2013

TEAM MEMBERS:	BEER BREWED:	SHARE HOLDERS:	BREWDOG BARS:
224 + 1 Dog	53,500 HL	14,208	13

Equity For Punks III raised £4.25 million, smashing crowdfunding records and welcoming almost 10,000 new investors. Meanwhile, we recorded Season 1 of our TV show 'Brew Dogs', featuring America's best craft brewers. Back on this side of the pond, we opened our first international bar in Stockholm with a funeral for generic beer and were both flattered and bemused when a fake BrewDog bar opened in China.

2014

TEAM MEMBERS:	BEER BREWED:	SHARE HOLDERS:	BREWDOG BARS:
358 + 1 Dog	90,000 HL	14,568	26

Our mission to spread the passion for craft beer continued with the opening of 12 new BrewDog bars as far afield as Brazil and Japan, as well as our first BottleDog and the awesome DogTap at BrewDog HQ. We released 36 different BrewDog beers, unleashed Truck Norris on the world, hit the screens with a second season of 'Brew Dogs' and made headlines for sticking it to Russian Premier, Vladimir Putin.

Hello, my name is Vladimir

2015

TEAM MEMBERS:	BEER BREWED:	SHARE HOLDERS:	BREWDOG BARS:
540 + 1 Dog	134,000 HL	32,000	44

We threw stuffed cats out of a helicopter over the bank of England to mark the launch of our latest round of Equity for Punks. We installed our first ever canning line at BrewDog HQ and we released the strongest canned ale in the world: Black Eyed King Imp. We took our business truly international opening BrewDog bars in Rome, Oslo, Brussels and Tokyo. And we made plans for our biggest venture yet – BrewDog Columbus USA.

2016

TEAM MEMBERS:	BEER BREWED:	SHARE HOLDERS:	BREWDOG BARS:
750 + 1 Dog	214,000 HL	55,000	50

As part of our commitment to transparency, with the revolutionary DIY Dog, we gave away the recipe in full for every single beer we had ever made. We also installed a new 300 HL (hectolitre) brewhouse in Ellon and built an amazing craft distillery. We also launched the amazing Elvis Juice, started building our new brewery in America and opened six great new BrewDog bars.

2017

TEAM MEMBERS:	BEER BREWED:	SHARE HOLDERS:	BREWDOG BARS:
1000 + 1 Dog	343,253 HL	70,000	56

To mark our first decade, we rewrote the blueprint for 21st century business with The Unicorn Fund, pledging to give away 10% of our profits evenly every year to all of our awesome crew members. We grew our global community to over 70,000 with Equity for Punks V, started brewing in Columbus and announced plans for a new BrewDog brewery in Brisbane, Australia. We also hit the *Sunday Times* Fast Track 100 for a record-breaking sixth year in a row. We also brewed the first ever batch of Hazy Jane, with the beer being a firm favourite ever since.

2018

TEAM MEMBERS:	BEER BREWED:	SHARE HOLDERS:	BREWDOG BARS:
1500 + 1 Dog	494,989 HL	96,000	81

We opened the world's first craft beer experiential hotel – The Doghouse – next to our Columbus brewery, as well as our very own beer museum on site too.

We smashed the world record for Equity crowdfunding with Equity for Punks V and launched the BrewDog Blueprint – a manifesto for the future of BrewDog. And we launched the first BrewDog Overworks beers from our custom-built sour beer brewery at BrewDog HQ.

2019

TEAM MEMBERS:	BEER BREWED:	SHARE HOLDERS:	BREWDOG BARS:
+2000 + 1 Dog	700,000 HL target	100,000+	90+

In September, we opened an amazing brewery and tap room in the heart of Berlin in a historic gasworks building dating back to 1901. We also finished building our new beautiful new brewery in Brisbane, Australia. Both of these new breweries helped us brew our beer closer to our customers and fans. Our Doghouse Hotel in Columbus was named one of the best 100 places on the planet (wow!) by TIME magazine and we continued to build our community all across Europe with Equity for Punks VI.

2020
& BEYOND . . .

Our first 12 years have been a pretty crazy ride.
Here's to the next 12 . . .

SECTION 2. SECTION 2. SECTION 2. SECTION 2.

Section 2
BREWDOG BITES

THE ORIGINAL BREWDOG

The original BrewDog is sadly no longer with us. The founding pup was James' dad's Chocolate Labrador called Bracken. He was the inspiration for the company name and was a star of many of our original videos. His favourite beer was 5am Saint, although he was usually more interested in stealing our brewers' lunches!

MOTHER FUCKER DAY

Annoyed at people saying that we were not punk enough anymore, a long standing team member decided to take matters into his own hands and coded 'Mother Fucker Day' onto the bottom of 200,000 cans causing retailer fury and a huge product recall.

In most businesses the person responsible for going rogue like this would be disciplined or fired. We made Graeme Wallace our employee of the month for April.

SUNK PUNK

We paid tribute to our nautical roots by fermenting an entire batch of Punk IPA at the bottom of the North Atlantic, making Sunk Punk the first ever beer brewed at the bottom of the ocean.

KICKSTARTING A REVOLUTION

To officially launch Equity for Punks III, and kickstart the craft beer revolution with a bang, we drove a tank through the streets of London and handed out samples of Punk IPA.

BREWDOG VS DIAGEO

Diageo cheating us out of an award in 2011 caused a global outcry and helped really put BrewDog on the map. Turns out revenge was a dish best served a few years later, in an Aberdeenshire swimming pool in a two man horse costume.

MY NAME IS ELVIS

The Elvis Presley Trust sued us for using Elvis' name on one of our beers and demanded a licence fee for every can we sold. Martin and myself (James) both legally changed our name to Elvis and sent them a letter back asking them for a licence fee for using our name on all of their music.

Case closed.

MEAN TWEETS

We decided to make the most out of the 'lovely' things people say about us on social media by getting the best quotes printed on our crew t-shirts. The t-shirts went viral and are now worn by our staff in 'shit hipster Wetherspoons' across the country.

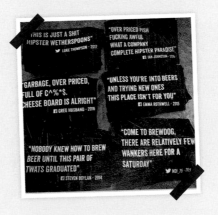

HELLO, MY NAME IS VLADIMIR

This one-off brew was a protest against the Kremlin's homophobic policies. We even dispatched a case of the beer to Moscow. And of course, we launched this beer with me, half naked on a horse.

YOUR CALL

In 2018 we launched an explosive marketing initiative entitled 'Your Call'. The posters compared our own Ratebeer.com scores with the scores of the biggest beer brands on the planet. All designed to highlight the massive quality difference between craft beer and macro beer.

MAKE EARTH GREAT AGAIN

We took a stand against Donald Trump pulling out of the Paris Agreement on Climate Change the only way we knew how – by brewing a beer and pouring it from a replica life-sized polar bear.

Make Earth Great Again was a 7.5% belgian ale brewed with water from melted polar ice caps. All proceeds of the beer were donated to 10:10, a charity lobbying for legislative changes relating to global warming.

SECTION 3. SECTION 3. SECTION 3. SECTION 3.

Section 3

SIGNATURE BREWDOG BENEFITS

At BrewDog we believe in always striving to be the best possible company that we can be to work for.

And we fully believe that our long-term destiny will be determined by how well we look after our amazing people.

We offer a host of exceptional core benefits from extra holiday days to enhanced pension contribution, from private medical care to a monthly beer allowance.

In addition, we offer a few signature BrewDog perks too, including:

- The Unicorn Fund

- Pawternity Leave

- Cicerone Training

- Free Sabbaticals

- The BrewDog Foundation

- The BrewDog Salary Cap

All of these killer perks look to reinforce the key things we believe in across our entire business and makes sure we are a great business to work for.

THE UNICORN FUND

Via our groundbreaking Unicorn Fund we share 10% of our profits evenly and every year with our entire team. It does not matter what your role, length of service or pay level is, everyone in the business is united by our truly democratic Unicorn Fund and everyone shares in our profit in the same way.

Our Unicorn Fund empowers all of our amazing team to act like business owners by rewarding them like business owners.

As part of the Unicorn Fund we also practise open book management, sharing our full financials with our entire team, every month.

PAWTERNITY LEAVE

We know that welcoming a four-legged arrival to the family is a big commitment. Gaining trust, housetraining and working out routines takes time, so we have decided to make things easy by offering Puppy Leave. It's like Parental Leave, but with more throwing of sticks. Take on a new dog (either puppy or a rescue dog) and you can have a week away from work to help your new family member settle in. We also allow dogs in our offices, so they'll never be too far away!

CICERONE TRAINING

Our mission is to make others as passionate about great craft beer as we are and elevate the status of beer. Both of these objectives are grounded in a deep knowledge of beer which underpins everything we do.

Cicerone set the benchmark for world class beer education and we have been working with them since 2010. We pay for the exams and everyone gets an automatic pay increase for every level they pass.

We have more Cicerone qualified beer experts in BrewDog than in any other company on the planet.

FREE SABBATICALS

Exploration, travel, learning and development are key cornerstones of anyone's personal journey. To that end, everyone who works for us for five years automatically qualifies for a fully paid four-week sabbatical to explore, to learn, to develop, to travel or just to chill.

Our team's sabbatical adventures so far include a road trip visiting every brewery on the West Coast of America, a trip across Australia and New Zealand, and even one person who took their baby on a tour of Belgian breweries!

THE BREWDOG FOUNDATION

We are committed to donating a portion of our profits each year to fund incredible charitable activities across the world. We are on a mission to change the world of beer, and we want to help you change the world at large. Through the BrewDog Foundation, we will donate £1 million each year to charitable initiatives that our crew want to support, we match fund our team members in their personal fundraising and we pay for our team members to work one day per year in a charity of their choice. This alone accounts to almost 2,000 days of work each year.

THE BREWDOG SALARY CAP

To these ends, we have the BrewDog Salary Cap. The BrewDog salary cap means that no one can join our business for a salary which is more than 7x what our entry level position is paid. Furthermore, this is capped at a maximum of 14x, increasing by one for each year of service.

This means we have to develop our own leaders internally and guarantees ample progression opportunities for our amazing team members in a new type of business, one that rejects the status quo and turns normal business assumptions on their head.

This is craft beer for the people, by the people.

SECTION 4. SECTION 4. SECTION 4. SECTION

Section 4

OUR CHARTER:

THE THINGS THAT WE BELIEVE IN

Our Mission is to make other people as passionate about great craft beer as we are. Our mission defines everything.

Our BrewDog Charter outlines what we believe in. It is our core DNA.

These are the things we
believe in.

These are the things that
we work for, that we strive
for, that we fight for.

These are the things that
underpin everything we do.

The BrewDog Charter was built with our team. Our Charter is our compass, it guides us, keeps us on course and importantly also holds us to account.

We are on a mission to make
other people as passionate
about great beer as we are.

We make things that we love.
Ourselves. From scratch.

We are community owned
and fiercely independent.

We believe in being a great
employer.

We want to show that business
can be a force for good.

OUR MISSION IS TO MAKE OTHER PEOPLE AS PASSIONATE ABOUT GREAT CRAFT BEER AS WE ARE.

World class craft beer is our true north.

HOW WE LIVE THIS:

We do all we can to get our beer into as many people's hands as possible.

We have almost 100 amazing craft beer bars all over the world.

We offer free beer schools to everyone.

We have more Cicerone-trained team members than any other company on the planet.

We give away all of our beer recipes with DIY Dog.

We support smaller brewers through the BrewDog Development Fund.

WE MAKE THINGS THAT WE LOVE. OURSELVES. FROM SCRATCH.

If we don't love it. We don't do it. Ever.

HOW WE LIVE THIS:

We build things from the ground up. From hotels to bars and from breweries to distilleries, we build things.

We brew our all of own beers at our ten brewery locations globally.

We also make amazing craft spirits.

And we make our own cider.

WE ARE COMMUNITY OWNED AND FIERCELY INDEPENDENT.

We are making a stand for independence, a stand for authenticity and a stand for craft.

HOW WE LIVE THIS:

We are part owned by a community of over 100,000 Equity Punks.

After one year, all of our team members become shareholders.

We have entrenched our independence into our articles of association.

We help support other independent businesses and promote independently brewed beer.

WE BELIEVE IN BEING A GREAT EMPLOYER

Our future depends on how well we look after
our amazing people.

HOW WE LIVE THIS:
We are a real living wage employer.

We share our profits with our team members.

We offer an amazing suite of employee benefits.

We focus on developing our own leaders
internally.

We have Pawternity leave for all team members.

WE WANT TO SHOW THAT BUSINESS CAN BE A FORCE FOR GOOD.

We believe in doing things differently and we believe in giving back.

HOW WE LIVE THIS:
Via our BrewDog Foundation which supports
causes chosen by our teams and our community.

Through our charity days and charity match
initiatives.

By looking after the environment.

By practising radical transparency and pioneering
our transparency dashboard.

By not being scared to take a stand for the things
we believe in.

OH AND GHOSTS. WE TOTALLY BELIEVE IN GHOSTS TOO. DON'T JUDGE.

SECTION 5. SECTION 5. SECTION 5. SECTION 5. SECTION

Section 5

THE BREWDOG DOGMAS

Martin and I set up BrewDog ten years ago with two humans, one dog and a big mission to change the world of beer. Our approach has been non-conformative and anti-authoritarian from the word go as we tore up the rule book and did things on our own terms.

It is vitally important we stay true to the ethos and the principles that have gotten us this far.

The BrewDog Dogmas are our road map, the detailed path, the blue print for taking ownership and taking the world by storm.

Whilst the Charter acts as our compass, our BrewDog Dogmas is more of a road map, the detailed path, the framework for decision making and a modern manual for being a 21st century business vigilante.

If the Charter is who we are, then the Dogmas are how we do things.

Our journey so far has been as unorthodox as it is remarkable. To ensure that continues, we need to continue to make unorthodox and remarkable decisions. The Dogmas help us do just that.

#1

IT IS ALWAYS DAY 1

As an underdog we need to live in start up mode.
We are happy being scrappy.

#2

BE CUSTOMER OBSESSED

Everything needs to start with the customer,
and work backwards.

We can only succeed long term by exceeding our
customers expectations time and time again.

#3

OWN YOUR NUMBERS

We need to fixate relentlessly on the numbers
which are key to our business.

What gets measured gets managed.

And what gets ignored sinks the ship.

#4

BE WHERE THE ACTION IS

The closer to the action we are, the
better decisions we will make.
Dogs not on deck are dead dogs.

#5

BE RADICALLY HONEST

Courageously candid conversations, direct feedback and vigorous debates are key to our culture and key to our future.

#6

SWEAT THE SMALL STUFF

The best teams fight for the small things
every day.

Because if the small things slide, then the
business falls apart.

#7

COUNT TIME IN DOG YEARS

The standard pace is for chumps.

Time is not money. It is way more important than that.

#8

BE UNCOMPROMISING

As a leader, unless people think your standards are unreasonably high, they are not high enough.

Every single bar needs to be set sky high.

#9

CHALLENGE EVERYTHING

We simply cannot accept things at face value.

We need to find our own path. And to find our own path we need to challenge everything. Hard.

#10

DO STUFF

We need to do stuff. Not speak about stuff.
Not plan stuff. Not have meetings about stuff.
We need to do stuff.

Talking about things gets us nowhere.
Action delivers results.

SECTION 6. SECTION 6. SECTION 6. SECTION 6.

Section 6

THE FIELD GUIDE TO . . .

#1

The Field Guide to . . .

GREAT MEETINGS

Maximum 30 minutes.

No mercy invites.

Clear agenda distributed in advance.

End with clear, timebound action points with owners.

And ask anyone using an electronic device to leave.

#2

The Field Guide to . . .

HIRING

We should do all that we can to avoid hiring anyone at all.

Striving to do more with less and developing the great people already on our team is always preferable to hiring.

If we HAVE to hire, be painstaking here: deciding who is in and who is out is the most important thing we do.

#3

The Field Guide to . . .

THE BREWDOG FOCUS TEST

1) Is it completely aligned with our Charter?

2) Can we do it better than anyone else in the world?

If the answer to either is no, then we should not waste our time.

#4

The Field Guide to . . .

CHAOS

Chaos and pressure are privileges.
Act accordingly.

#5

The Field Guide to . . .

SPENDING MONEY

Spend every single penny of BrewDog's money
as if you were reaching deep into your own
pocket and spending your own
hard-earned cash . . .

#6

The Field Guide to . . .

IMPROVEMENT

If you can't measure it. You can't improve it.

#7

The Field Guide to . . .

TOUGH CONVERSATIONS

Clear is kind. Unclear is unkind.

#8

The Field Guide to . . .

INNOVATION

The goal is always to kill our business.

#9

The Field Guide to . . .

BAD APPLES

Eliminate them quickly.
Zero tolerance.

#10

The Field Guide to . . .

POLICIES

Policies are organisational scar tissue.
We should not scar on the first cut.

#11

The Field Guide to . . .

A PROBLEM

The problem is never the problem.
The problem is always people's attitude
towards the problem.

#12

The Field Guide to . . .

HATERS

Getting people to hate you is easy.
All you need to do is to be successful
doing something you love.

#13

The Field Guide to . . .

HARD THINGS

The hard thing always creates the value.
It is supposed to be difficult.

If it were easy, everyone would do it.

#14

The Field Guide to . . .

SUCCESS

Nothing recedes like success.
We need to earn it every single day.

Only the paranoid win.

#15

The Field Guide to . . .

BEING REASONABLE

Being reasonable is the most common path to mediocrity.

#16

The Field Guide to . . .

ZIP-LINING THROUGH THE BREWERY

Only do this after at least four beers, and if you intend to post it on social media.

#17

The Field Guide to . . .

TIMESCALES

Everyone will be queuing up to dictate
the timescale of a project to us.

But it is:

- Our business
- Our brand
- Our money
- Our team

And therefore OUR timeline.
And we have zero time to waste.

#18

The Field Guide to . . .

FIGHTING OUR CORNER

We all need to have an extraordinarily high bullshit filter and a stubborn, bordering on maniacal, refusal to accept the wrong answer or the wrong result.

If we don't fight, we lose by default.

#19

The Field Guide to . . .

FLATNESS

Screw traditional corporate hierarchies.
We need to keep our world as flat as possible. Every
manager should aim for at least ten direct reports.
Any less is too hierarchical for how we operate.

#20

The Field Guide to . . .

CHANGE

Be excited for change.
Be wary of the smoke of nostalgia.

#21

The Field Guide to . . .

PROJECTS

The quality of output of a project:

a) is inversely proportional to the number of people involved.

b) increases in direct proportion to the involvement of the ultimate decision maker.

#22

The Field Guide to . . .

SIMPLICITY

Simple is much harder than complex.

Complex solutions are usually the outcome of
second rate thinking.

#23

The Field Guide to . . .

THINKING
SMALL

'If we think small and act small, we'll get bigger. If we think big and act big, we'll get smaller.' Herb Kelleher

Thinking small needs to be an obsession for us.

24

The Field Guide to . . .

THE RESOURCE CURSE

The more resources on a project, the poorer
the outcome usually is.

#25

The Field Guide to . . .

GREAT
BRANDS

Do remarkable things.
Have a healthy disdain for the status quo.
Refuse to settle for good enough.
Become great through tough decisions and
overcoming obstacles.

COMFORT
ZONE

#26

The Field Guide to . . .

COMFORT ZONES

Comfort zones are places where ordinary
people do mediocre things.

YOU

#27

The Field Guide to . . .

CULTURE

Culture is the by-product of consistent behaviour. Words (and the words in this book) are essentially useless unless we live them.

SECTION 7. SECTION 7. SECTION 7. SECTION 7. SECTION 7. SECTION

Section 7
HOLD FAST

Our journey so far has been as crazy as it has been remarkable. We are an anomaly, a glitch in the matrix. And we need to stay that way.

We certainly did not get here by being normal, by playing it safe, by conforming. We got here by being fast, tenacious, passionate and by putting everything on the line for what we believe in time and time again.

Very few growing companies manage to make the transition from small company to medium sized company and keep their culture intact. The companies which manage to fight hard enough to keep their culture as they grow end up becoming iconic and enduring global businesses – like Patagonia, like Netflix, like Google and like Southwest Airlines.

We need to ensure we fight hard enough for the things we believe in and the things we love so that we can remain an anomaly.

Together, we can set a new standard for beer and for business on a global scale and build one of the best companies of our generation.

Hold Fast,
BrewDog x

We are in the driving seat of the beer industry.

So let's grip the wheel. And drive it like we fucking stole it.

APPENDICES

Appendix 1: *How to fuck BrewDog up. Royally.*

1. Losing focus on the beer.
2. Thinking big.
3. Taking customers for granted.
4. Not listening to our community.
5. Hiding from issues.
6. Accepting anything but unreasonably high standards.
7. Being complacent.
8. Accepting things at face value.
9. Hiring too many people.
10. Dumbing things down.

Appendix 2: *Life Advice from the Mad Hatter*

Safe is boring. Safe gets lost. Safe blends into anonymous mediocrity. We take risks.

We specialise in unheard of things.

The Mad Hatter liked to believe in six impossible things before breakfast. We need to do the same.

Notes

_____

_____

_____

_____

_____

_____

_____

_____

_____

_____

_____

_____

_____

_____

_____

_____